S1

# Amazing Animal Books
# For Young Readers

**Nadine Thiele**
**Mendon Cottage Books**

*JD-Biz Publishing*

## Download Free Books!
## http://MendonCottageBooks.com

### Read More Amazing Animal Books

# Table of Contents

# About Snakes

Did you know that snakes are one of the most misunderstood creatures in the animal kingdom? In this book we are going to learn about snakes. We are going to talk about where they live, how they hunt, what they eat, and learn some fun and interesting facts about snakes. One thing that is very interesting about snakes is that some species lay eggs to hatch and other species give birth to live young. As we talk about each different snake keep an eye out for which ones lay eggs and which have live babies. Snakes are also grouped together in different families just like humans! We will learn a few of the snake families and some of the snakes that belong to them.

# Boa Snakes, Water Snakes

The largest snake family is the Colubridae. They include almost 70% of all snakes and can be found worldwide. Snakes in this family group lay eggs or sometimes have live babies. Animals that give birth to live babies are called viviparous and animals that lay eggs are called oviparous.

The next family of snakes in this book is the Elapidae. They are a venomous snake which means they inject their prey with poison through their fangs. They live mostly in tropical, wet areas and almost all of them lay eggs. One type of Elapidae is the Sea Snake which is different than the Water Snake.

# Pythons and Rattlesnakes

One of the more interesting families of snakes is the Boidae. They are typically non-venomous and what's interesting about them is that they are constrictors. They do not inject their prey with venom. Instead they wrap their bodies around the prey and compress the victim until it suffocates. Some scientists consider pythons to part of this family. Scientists who study snakes have their own special name. They are called herpetologists. Sometimes they can be called serpentologists. If you were going to study snakes which name would you choose?

The last family of snakes that we are going to learn about in this book is the Viperidae. Remember these are only a few of the snake families. There are many more that you can learn about. Viperidae refers to viper and the snakes in this family are venomous. Rattlesnakes belong in this family and we will talk about some of them as well as others.

# Venomous Snakes

Before we move on to any particular type of snake let's take a moment to look at snake fangs. There are two types of fangs that snakes can have. First they can have hollow fangs that work like a needle and inject their poisonous venom right into their victim. Second, they can have solid fangs that bite their prey but the venom slowly drips down onto the bite. Not all snakes have fangs but almost all snakes do have teeth. Sometimes a snake's fang breaks off during an attack or bite. When this happens it will grow another one back.

The picture above is of a Gaboon Viper. They have the longest fangs of all of the vipers. The fangs on the Gaboon Viper can grow up to two inches long!

The Desert Adder lives in Australia. It has long fangs and is very poisonous. It is mostly active at night. They eat lizards and rodents. The Desert Adder attracts its prey by shimmying the tip of its tail as it lies in the sand. They will lie in the sand for days at a time while they lure in their prey. They also give birth to live young.

Let's move on to the Red Beaked Snake-sometimes called the Rufous Beaked Snake. They are mostly active during the day and usually grow up to 3 ½ feet long. They prefer to live in bushes and trees and eat small animals. They are considered to be a mildly venomous snake and they also give birth to live young.

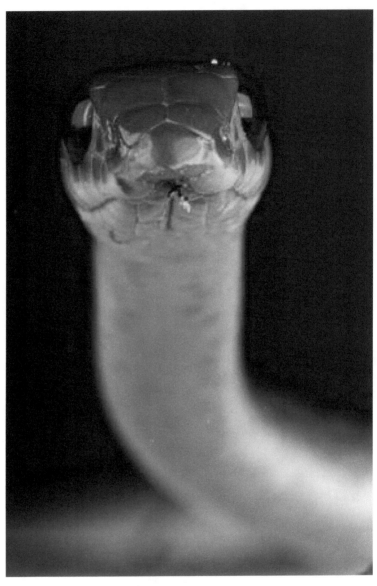

**Red Beaked Snake**

The Coastal Taipan is particularly venomous member of the Elapidaes. They are most common in Australia but also live in New Guinea. Have you noticed how many snakes live in Australia? The

Coastal Taipan grows up to almost 7 feet long. They are active in the early morning and the early evening. Their diet is small rodents, insects, and other animals.

**Coastal Taipan**

# Corn Snakes

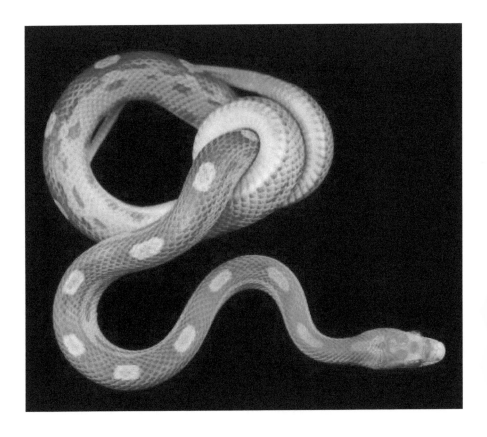

The Corn Snake is a constrictor that is commonly kept as a pet. They grow from between 4-6 feet in length. In nature Corn Snakes prefer thick foliage or fields and are most lively during the day. In the wild a corn snake will eat rodents and bird eggs but in captivity they normally eat mice. They are a non-venomous snake.

# Cobras

The snake pictured here is the Spitting Cobra. The Spitting Cobra does not "spit" its venom but instead sprays it out through its fangs giving it the appearance of spitting. It is one of the largest venomous snakes and grows to about 10-13 feet long. It expands its jaws to swallow prey much larger than its own head. The Spitting Cobra would rather live near water than anywhere else and eats a varied diet of lizards, birds, rodents and frequently ratsnake.

# Most Dangerous Snakes

One of the most notorious types of snake is the Black Mamba Snake. They can grow up to 8 feet long. Black mambas are not named for the color of their bodies. They are named for the color on the inside of their mouth. They are one of the fastest snakes in the world and can move up to 12 miles per hour! Most often they use their speed to flee from humans rather than to hurt them. They live in many different climates but they do prefer dry areas. They eat many different animals.

Members of the Elapidae family have hollow fangs that inject their venom like a hypodermic needle. The close up picture shows a Black Mamba in the midst of an attack. Look closely to see the black color inside its mouth.

There are many legends and stories surrounding the Black Mamba. It has a very viscous reputation and many people are fearful of the Black Mamba. Its venom is highly toxic to humans but if a person who is bit receives medicine in time they will often recover.

# Dangerous Snakes

Similar to the Black Mamba is the Green Mamba. It is much less aggressive than its relative though. The Green Mamba can usually be found in trees and is more active during the day. They are normally about 5 feet long. Green Mambas lay eggs. They eat lizards, other snakes, birds, bird eggs and rodents.

**Green Mamba**

The next viperidae is called the Saharan Sand Viper. This is a nocturnal snake. This snake is almost always found in the sand and is very well known for its side winding movements. The Sand Vipers lay eggs. They eat lizards and rodents at night after hiding under the sand during the heat of the day.

**Saharan Sand Viper**

# King Snakes

When someone is talking about a King Snake sometimes they are talking about a King Cobra and sometimes they are talking about the type of Kingsnake you see here. This Kingsnake is a Colubridae. They can be found mostly in Florida and along the eastern coast of the United States. They are happy in different kinds of environments but they especially like swamps, forests and wetlands. They are mostly active during the day and they eat small animals. The Kingsnake is a constrictor. They lay eggs and grow up to about 3 ½ feet long. The Kingsnake is sometimes kept as a pet.

# White Snakes

Once in a while a snake is born with no pigment or color in its skin. This is called an albino snake. These snakes are not always pure white, however they typically do have red eyes. Any species of animal can produce albino offspring. The snake in this picture is an albino rattlesnake.

# Rattlesnakes

The Western Diamondback Rattlesnake can be over 39 inches long. It is also known as the Red Rattlesnake and is extremely venomous. They are the most well-known rattlesnakes perhaps because they can be found in many types of habitats. They prefer cool, dry areas. They eat lizards, rabbits, squirrels and birds. Diamondbacks give birth to live young.

# Molting

A new rattle is added each time the snake molts or sheds its skin. However, occasionally these rattles will break off so it is not necessarily a good way to tell a rattlesnakes age. The picture shown here is probably not from a rattlesnake but all snakes, no matter what the species, must shed their skins to grow.

The skin of a snake is very important. It works just like a human's skin to keep out diseases and parasites. Oftentimes a snakeskin also helps the snake when it is trying to move and it helps to keep the snake hydrated. A few times a year a snake will shed its skin which is called "molting." Most people don't understand how important molting is for a snake. When a snake sheds its skin it's shedding all of the parasites and infections it may have picked up in the time since its last molt.

# Rat Snakes

Also among the Colubridaes is the Green Rat Snake. They live in many areas including woodlands and mountains. They enjoy living in the rainforest and can often be found in the trees hanging from the branches. They normally eat birds, bird eggs and bats. This is a type of snake that lays eggs. It is also non-venomous but it is a constrictor.

# Black Snakes

Many snakes could be classified as "Black Snakes." Among them are a few we've already seen including some of the Kingsnakes and even to a few people the Black Mamba in spite of the fact that the Black Mamba is not truly a black snake.

Let's take a look at the Mangrove Snake. They can be found in trees or on the ground and most people call them "cat snakes" because of the way their head is shaped. These snakes grow up to about 5 feet long. They are considered a nocturnal snake. That means they are mostly active at night. They mainly eat lizards, birds, rodents, fish and even other snakes. They are mildly venomous.

The Black Tiger Snake is another venomous snake that belongs to the Elapidaes. It lives is Australia and can grow up to 7 feet long. Remember how we learned most of the Elapidae lay eggs? This is one of the members of the family that actually gives birth to live young. They prefer to live in wet areas and eat mostly birds.

# Scrub Python

The Scrub Python is another constrictor. An ordinary male will grow to about 10 feet long. Another characteristic (or feature) of these snakes is that they are quite slender for a constrictor. They are normally found in rainforests. They eat birds, possums, rats and fruit bats.

The Green Tree Python is another snake that lives in the rainforest. They grow to about 5 ½ feet long and they eat small animals such as rodents and reptiles including other snakes. Sometimes the Green Tree Python is kept as a pet but they take a lot of work. They need a special cage providing heat, moisture, and of course the right food.

# Boas

The Emerald Tree Boa is very common in rainforests. They are born live and can grow up to six feet long. Emerald Tree Boas eat many things including lizards, frogs and birds. These snakes are well-known for hanging and draping themselves around the branches of the rainforest trees.

The Tartar Sand Boa is another type of snake in this family. There is actually not very much information available about it. Information that is known about this snake includes its diet. It mostly eats rodents and once in awhile a lizard or maybe a bird. It also lives in the sand and gives birth to live young.

The Woma is an Australian Boidae. They are an endangered species of snake. The word endangered means that there are very few of them left on our planet. There are many people who devote their time to make sure those animals who are in danger of becoming extinct are protected so they can continue to thrive. The Woma is a nocturnal snake. Do you remember what nocturnal is? That's right! That means they are active at night. They mostly eat lizards, rodents and birds.

**Snake Eating a Frog**

# Garter Snakes

Next we're going to talk about the Common Garter Snake. This snake lives almost anywhere. They can be found in almost any habitat and are not picky about the climate. They are usually most active during the day and normally grow up to 22 inches long. They give birth to live young and their diet consists of insects, worms, and sometimes even small fish.

**Garter Snake**

The Blue Ribbon Snake is also a type of Colubridae. It is non-venomous and very common in Florida. They especially like to live in wet areas. They grow to about 18-25 inches in length. Many snake lovers enjoy keeping this type of snake as a pet. They eat worms, slugs, insects and sometimes minnows. They also have live young.

**Blue Ribbon Snake**

Last is the Water Snake. They are non-venomous. That means that they do not have poison in their fangs. They are active during the day and the night which is unusual for a snake. They eat almost anything, including; minnows, worms, fish, and frogs. They are also a type of snake that gives birth to live young.

**Water Snake**

# How Can I Help?

As you can see there are some very exciting and fun things you can learn about snakes. Snakes are very important for our environment. They provide food for many animals including other snakes, birds and alligators. They also help control populations of other animals such as insects. Without snakes the amount of insects, rodents and other animals may get out of control. They are a priceless part of our ecosystem.

The snake's most deadly enemy, however, is humans. Humans have been known to hunt snakes for their skin. It is used to make wallets, purses and shoes among other things. People also destroyed the snakes' natural habitat in many areas and in other places sometimes snakes are killed because people are scared. This is especially true in the case of the Black Mamba which has many myths and legends surrounding it.

Sometimes snakes are captured and used to make what is called antivenin. Antivenin is medicine that is made from the poisonous venom inside the snake. It is used to cure snakebite victims and save lives.

Last but not least sometimes snakes are taken out of their natural environment to be kept as pets.

Now that we know about these problems what can we do?

- The most important thing you can do to help is not to buy products made of snakeskin. If you see products made out of snakeskin do not support that company!

If you are interested in having a snake (or any king of reptile as a pet) make sure to purchase it from a good pet dealer and that you know how to take care of it properly. Many people are attracted to the idea of having a snake as a pet but once they purchase it they find that it is not what they thought it would be and they do not know how to care for their new pet. Do your research. Make sure that you have the time to invest in your new pet and the resources to feed it.

There are resources online and in your local community that you can join that support endangered species and can help you learn more about saving and preserving the environment. One of them is www.endangeredspeciesinternational.org

Finally, don't forget what you can do close to you. Put your garbage in the trash. Walk if you can and make an effort to recycle. These little everyday changes will make a big difference to all animals everywhere.

# Fun Facts About Snakes

As we end our journey with snakes let's look at some fun facts about them.

1) Snakes do not have eyelids. A transparent layer protects the eye.

2) During each and every year the snake sheds its skin for about 10 times which lasts for about a week.

3) Snakes do not bite their food instead they swallow their prey in one mouth. They also have jaws that are flexible so they can swallow anything which is bigger than them also.

4) Snakes do have external ears. They contain only internal ears.

5) They smell with their tongue because they do not have a nose.

6) Snakes can swim .Some snakes swim on the surface of the water while some snakes even swim underwater.

7) Some snakes can camouflage themselves to protect themselves from its enemies.

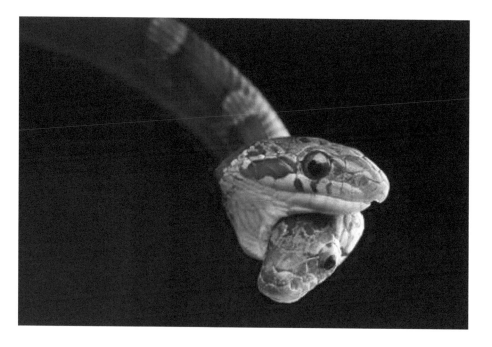

**Pictured here is a two headed snake. Two headed snakes occur when the embryo inside the egg doesn't fully divide. This can happen in any species but is most normally seen in snakes and turtles.**

8) There are more than 3000 different species present around the world.

9) They can breathe through their skin when they are underwater.

10) Snakes sometimes use venom to hurt thier victims.

**All Images Licensed by Fotolia.com**

Cover Photo

Green ratsnake / Gonyosoma oxycephalum

© *mgkuijpers - Fotolia.com*

Two headed snake

© *mgkuijpers - Fotolia.com*

Saharan Sand Viper / Cerastes vipera

© *mgkuijpers - Fotolia.com*

Red rattlesnake / Crotalus ruber

© *mgkuijpers - Fotolia.com*

Albino rattlesnake

© *mgkuijpers - Fotolia.com*

Western Diamondback Rattlesnake (Crotalus atrox)

© *Steve Byland - Fotolia.com*

Adult boa, which lies in the aquarium.

© *seleznyov - Fotolia.com*

Coastal Taipan / Oxyuranus scutellatus

© *mgkuijpers - Fotolia.com*

Desert adder / Bitis peringuey

© *mgkuijpers - Fotolia.com*

King cobra / Ophiophagus hannah

© *mgkuijpers - Fotolia.com*

Attacking Black mamba / Dendroaspis polylepis

© *mgkuijpers - Fotolia.com*

---

Green mamba / Dendroaspis angusticeps

Black tiger snake / Telescopus dhara

Spitting cobra / Naja sputatrix

Green ratsnake / Gonyosoma oxycephalum

Common Garter Snake Thamnophis sirtalis

Red beaked snake / Rhampiophis rubropunctatus

Blue ribbon snake / Thamnophis sauritus

Water-Snake Out of the Water

Mangrove snake / Boiga dendrophila

Attacking rat snake / Orthriophis taeniurus

Shed Snakeskin (32382002)

## References

www. nationalzoo.si.edu/animals/reptilesamphibians

www.desertmuseum.org

www.thebigzoo.com/zoo/squamata/asp

www.dnr.state.mn.us › Nature › Animals › Reptiles / Amphibians

animals.nationalgeographic.com/animals/reptiles

http://ufwildlife.ifas.ufl.edu

http://www.wikipedia.org/

# About the Author

Nadine Thiele was born in Edmonton, Alberta, Canada. She spent much of her childhood there before she moved to Minnesota to complete school and college. That is where she met and married her husband. She still lives in Minnesota and enjoys spending time with her family and her pets. She enjoys reading and writing. One of her favorite hobbies is volunteering to read with the local children who often are just learning English as they move to the area from other educational backgrounds.

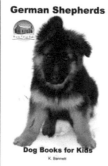

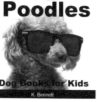

Our books are available at

1. Amazon.com
2. Barnes and Noble
3. Itunes
4. Kobo
5. Smashwords
6. Google Play Books

# Download Free Books!
# http://MendonCottageBooks.com

# Publisher

JD-Biz Corp

P O Box 374

Mendon, Utah 84325

http://www.jd-biz.com/

CPSIA information can be obtained
at www.ICGtesting.com
Printed in the USA
BVHW011912180723
667438BV00002B/4